D0450581

"The Republican Caucus of the Virginia General Assembly censured *Doonesbury* cartoonist Garry Trudeau today for his satirical treatment of U.S. Sen. John Warner and his wife, actress Elizabeth Taylor.

"The censure motion was made by Sen. Wiley Mitchell of Alexandria. The Republican legislators, without dissent, voted to 'express our outrage and indignation' over the cartoon strip's treatment of Virginia's new GOP senator and his wife.

"Mitchell said at the caucus he was not blaming the newspaper editors for printing the strip, but that he believed Virginia Republican legislators should let Trudeau know they consider the Warner-Taylor satire 'outrageously offensive to good taste and common decency.'"

—*Associated Press*

Bantam Books by G.B. Trudeau
Ask your bookseller for the books you have missed

A TAD OVERWEIGHT, BUT VIOLET EYES TO DIE FOR
"ANY GROOMING HINTS FOR YOUR FANS, ROLLIE?"
"BUT THE PENSION FUND WAS JUST SITTING THERE"
CALL ME WHEN YOU FIND AMERICA
DARE TO BE GREAT, MS. CAUCUS
AN ESPECIALLY TRICKY PEOPLE
JOANIE
"SPEAKING OF INALIENABLE RIGHTS, AMY..."
STALKING THE PERFECT TAN
WE'RE NOT OUT OF THE WOODS YET
"WHAT DO WE HAVE FOR THE WITNESSES,
    JOHNNIE?"
WOULDN'T A GREMLIN HAVE BEEN MORE SENSIBLE?
YOU'RE NEVER TOO OLD FOR NUTS AND BERRIES

A Tad Overweight, but Violet Eyes to Die For

A *Doonesbury* Book

by G. B. Trudeau

BANTAM BOOKS

TORONTO · NEW YORK · LONDON · SYDNEY

A TAD OVERWEIGHT BUT VIOLET EYES TO DIE FOR

*A Bantam Book / published by arrangement with
Holt, Rinehart & Winston*

PRINTING HISTORY

Holt, Rinehart & Winston edition published March 1980

Bantam edition / August 1981

ISBN 0-553-14337-9

Published simultaneously in the United States and Canada

PRINTED IN THE UNITED STATES OF AMERICA

0 9 8 7 6 5 4 3 2 1

THANK YOU, ELIZA-
BETH! IF I MAY,
I'D LIKE TO MAKE
A TOAST TO OUR
NEW FRIENDS!

AS YOU KNOW, WE HAD
ORIGINALLY INTENDED TO
SPEND THE FALL "EATING
OUR WAY ACROSS FRANCE,"
AS ELIZABETH LIKES TO
PUT IT..

BUT FATE INTERVENED,
DUTY CALLED, AND NOW
HERE WE ARE IN WASH-
INGTON, ATTENDING
WONDERFUL PARTIES!

SO LET'S
DRINK TO
FUTURE PAR-
TIES! AND TO
THE SENATE,
TOO!

"THE
SENATE,
TOO?"

YOU WERE
RIGHT. HE
DOES HAVE
A SERIOUS
SIDE.

GBTrudeau

GOOD EVENING. I'M ROLAND HEDLEY BURTON, JR. TONIGHT, ".30/.30" EXAMINES ONE OF THE STRANGEST PHENOMENA IN RECENT POLITICAL HISTORY..

HIS NAME IS EDWARD MOORE KENNEDY. HE IS THE SENIOR SENATOR FROM MASSACHUSETTS. BUT TO HIS THOUSANDS OF DEVOTED FOLLOWERS, HE IS KNOWN SIMPLY AS "TED."

WHO ARE THESE FOLLOWERS? WHERE DO THEY COME FROM? WHAT FORCE DRIVES THEM TO THROW GOOD MONEY AFTER BAD? TONIGHT, ABC WIDE WORLD OF NEWS LOOKS AT..

"THE LIBERAL CULT: THREAT FROM THE LEFT!"

The Liberal Cult

news abc close-up

COMPASSION. JUSTICE. A FAIR SHAKE. THESE ARE THE PROFESSED GOALS OF THE KENNEDY "CULT OF CONSCIENCE."

AND YET, FOR ALL THE EGALITARIAN POSTURING OF THE LIBERALS, GATHERING SIGNS INDICATE THAT WITHIN THE CULT ITSELF, SOME ARE MORE EQUAL THAN OTHERS!

ABC NEWS HAS JUST LEARNED OF THE EXISTENCE OF AN INNER ELITE, A TIGHTLY KNIT CADRE OF LOYALISTS SO CLOSE TO "TED" THAT THEY'RE ACTUALLY RELATED TO HIM.

REFERRED TO AS THE KENNEDY "CLAN," THEIR EXACT NUMBER IS UNKNOWN..

OKAY, MR. DUKE, YOU'VE BEEN HERE BEFORE, SO I DON'T HAVE TO TELL YOU THAT THIS CONGRESS IS EVERY BIT AS SPINELESS AS ITS PREDECESSORS!

REMEMBER, THE LEGISLATORS WE DON'T OWN OUTRIGHT ARE SCARED TO DEATH OF MAIL! THEY'RE IN YOUR POCKET, MR. DUKE, SO WHEN YOU WALK THROUGH THAT DOOR, WALK TALL!

GOTCHA. I DON'T REALLY HAVE TO READ ALL OF THESE CRIME-STOPPER STORIES, DO I?

NO, NO, OF COURSE NOT. YOU JUST BE YOURSELF. YOU'RE OUR ACE IN THE HOLE, MR. DUKE!

I AM? WHAT HAPPENED TO THE WIDOW WHO WASTED NINE MUGGERS?

SHE FOLLOWS YOU. YOU'RE OUR NUMBER-ONE GUN!

AS YOU KNOW, DR. MAHDAVI, IN RECENT WEEKS, THERE HAS BEEN AN OUTPOURING OF PROTEST FROM IRANIAN WOMEN OVER THE ALL-COVERING "CHADOR," WHICH THEY SEE AS A SYMBOL OF ISLAMIC SEXISM.

WILL THE AYATOLLAH RESPOND TO THIS NEW..

IT HAS ALREADY BEEN RESOLVED. THE RULE ABOUT THE CHADOR WAS BEING TAKEN TOO LITERALLY.

THE AYATOLLAH DOES NOT DIS- APPROVE OF OTHER FORMS OF DRESS, AS LONG AS THEY ARE MODEST. WHAT HE DOES OBJECT TO ARE SKIRTS AND GOWNS, THE GARMENTS OF PROSTITUTES!

I SEE. HOW ABOUT THE ANNIE HALL LOOK?

IF WORN WITH A VEIL, FINE.

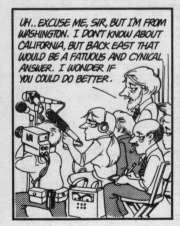

DAY, MAY 8, 1979

15

Californian Creates 'Context' For White House Bid

Vows Commitment To Public Mood

By Rick Redfern
SACRAMENTO,
California, May 7 –
Today, in a press
ference at t
rni

THE WASH...

Carter Symbol Chief to Defect

Cardigans Seen in Sacramento

By Rick Redfe

WASHINGTON,
May 7 – The W
Phonathon,
Tree House
Fireside C
said he w
ser

Secretary of Symbol-
ism Duane Delacourt

THE CAPITOL

THE WAS

Campaign '80:

Brown Assembles 'Mellow Mafia'

Tom Hayden, Others, to Sell Out

Analysis by
Rick Redfern

Governor Jerry Brown is
sometimes compared to a
Rorschach test; people
see in him what they
want. How else
to explain
th

B
uz
wor
buzz
words
buzz w
rds buz
word

MY, HAVEN'T WE BEEN A BUSY BOY!

WE NEED THE MONEY.

GB Trudeau

UH..ROLAND, IF YOU DON'T MIND, I'D LIKE TO GET THIS THING STARTED..

JUST ONE QUICK STAND-UP, BUDDY, AND WE'LL BE OUT OF YOUR WAY!

THIS IS ROLAND HEDLEY, JR., IN LOS ANGELES. TONIGHT, ABC NEWS LOOKS AT A SORDID STORY ABOUT THE TANGLED DESTINIES OF A GOVERNOR, A RACKETEER, AND A MOVIE TYCOON!

IT'S ALSO A STORY OF INFLUENCE AND FIXING, BUT HEY, LET'S LET THE GRAND JURY SORT THAT OUT! FOR NOW, LET'S LISTEN TO BROWN SPOKESMAN DUANE DELACOURT TRY TO DEFEND HIS BOSS!

UH..

THIRTY SECONDS, BUDDY.

ROLLING!

GBTrudeau